ANIMALS IN ORBIT

ANIMALS IN ORBIT

MONKEYNAUTS AND OTHER PIONEERS IN SPACE

KATHERINE McGLADE MARKO

FRANKLIN WATTS
NEW YORK   LONDON   TORONTO   SYDNEY
A FIRST BOOK
1991

Cover photograph courtesy of NASA

Photographs courtesy of: Sovfoto: pp. 2, 24 (both from Tass), 17, 19,
20; UPI/Bettmann Newsphotos: pp. 13, 16, 21, 26, 28, 29, 35, 37 bottom,
39, 41, 45, 53; N.A.S.A.: pp. 29 (insert), 33, 37 top, 45 (insert),
48, 49, 50, 54.

Library of Congress Cataloging-in-Publication Data

Marko, Katherine.
Animals in orbit : monkeynauts and other pioneers in space /
Katherine McGlade Marko.
p.   cm. — (A First book)
Includes bibliographical references and index.
Summary: Discusses the animals originally sent up in space as
experiments, and looks at current projects being conducted on
various plants and animals.
ISBN 0-531-20003-5
1. Space flight—Juvenile literature.   2. Dogs as laboratory
animals—Juvenile literature.   3. Monkeys as laboratory animals—
Juvenile literature.   4. Chimpanzees as laboratory animals—
Juvenile literature. [1. Space flight. 2. Dogs as laboratory
animals.   3. Monkeys as laboratory animals.   4. Chimpanzees as
laboratory animals.] I. Title. II. Series.
TL793.M315   1991
629.45–dc20   90-47226 CIP AC

To our grandson
Matthew John Marko

On the title page: A Soviet monkey "cosmonaut"
sits in a space probe simulator vessel.

The author wishes to extend a note of thanks to all
those on the staffs of NASA, Kennedy Space Center,
Florida and Washington, D.C.; Space Center, Alamogordo,
New Mexico; The Space & Rocket Center, Huntsville, Alabama;
Smithsonian Institution Zoological Park, Washington, D.C.; and
Lincoln Park Zoo, Chicago, Illinois, for their cordial answers
to questions and the valuable information rendered.

CONTENTS

ANIMALS IN ORBIT

INTRODUCTION

Long before anyone dreamed of exploring outer space, even before airplanes were invented, there were people who looked at the birds of the air and wished they could fly themselves.

Steps to fulfill this dream began more than two hundred years ago in France, where hydrogen balloons were being developed and perfected. Finally, a hot-air balloon, assembled by two brothers, Joseph-Michel and Jacques-Étienne Montgolfier, was ready for demonstration.

11

The brothers wanted a manned ascent for their balloon right away. But, because of the fears and superstitions of the day, the brothers met with great opposition. Chief among those against the idea of a manned flight was King Louis XVI himself. Much as people wanted to fly, two questions remained: Would it be safe for a living creature to be airborne? And what effect would soaring high above the earth have on the human body?

The brothers finally agreed to try sending animals up first. It was decided that a rooster, a duck, and a sheep would make the flight. Afterward, they would be checked for any ill effects.

On September 19, 1783, a great crowd gathered near the palace in Versailles. It took about ten minutes to fill the balloon with hot air in the palace yard. Then, while assistants held the ropes that kept the balloon earthbound, a large basket was fastened to its bottom. Into the basket went the rooster, the duck, and the sheep. The sheep, frightened by all the excitement, kicked wildly before settling down.

Finally, all was ready. As King Louis XVI and Queen Marie Antoinette watched, the assistants let go of the ropes and the bright blue and gold balloon rose grandly from its platform and soared away.

Astronomers in the crowd watched the balloon's ascent through their telescopes and reported its prog-

A flying hot-air balloon was a strange and exciting sight to the people of France during the late 1700s.

ress. Eventually it reached an altitude of about 1,600 feet (488 m). Eight minutes later, when the air inside the covering cooled, the balloon—the first vehicle to carry living creatures aloft—landed in the woods of Vaucresson, only two and one-half miles (4 km) from its launching point.

The impact on landing broke the basket open and the animals scurried away. All were unharmed by the flight.

The first flight to carry a live cargo was considered a success. To everyone's delight, the hot-air balloon was proof that a craft built by humans could fly. More important, the flight proved that living creatures could survive air travel.

THE SOVIET MUTTNIKS

In 1903 the Wright brothers invented the first airplane to be driven by a pilot.

The field of aviation grew rapidly. But no animals were sent up on flights for experiments. The only animals taken up in planes were those being transported somewhere.

In May 1927, Charles Lindbergh flew nonstop across the Atlantic Ocean. His flight from New York to Paris took thirty-three and one-half hours. It was a human triumph and people now knew that air travel had conquered the oceans.

15

In this classic 1927 photograph, Charles Lindbergh poses in front of the plane that took him across the Atlantic Ocean.

Once air travel became commonplace, people turned their attention toward outer space. But in outer space there is no air to breathe, and there is the problem of weightlessness because there is no gravity. Could a human being survive under such conditions?

Again animals served as trailblazers.

The United States was not the only nation interested in space exploration. The Soviet Union was, too, and they put the first artificial satellite, *Sputnik I,* into space. Next they planned to send up manned spacecraft, but were faced with the uncertainty of the effects of space travel on the human mind and body.

So they, too—like the balloon inventors of two hundred years before—decided to send up animals first.

In the mid 1950s the Soviets began to launch mongrel dogs into the lower reaches of space. Mongrels (dogs of mixed breeds) were chosen because they were more rugged and could withstand the rigors of space flight better than pedigreed, or purebred, dogs. It was also decided that only white females weighing no more than sixteen pounds (7.25 kg) would be used. White dogs were selected because they would photograph better for the film transmissions from space. The weight restriction was due to the size of the capsules that would rocket the animals into space.

Canine specialists searched Moscow for the dogs, some of which were bought and some obtained by other means.

The dogs were trained to get them used to the confinement of the capsule, special trays for food, sanitation equipment, and noise and vibrations. They

A "muttnik" is shown here modeling one of the earliest space suits designed by the Soviet space program.

were also conditioned to wait patiently for long periods of time.

It is said that the Russians flew at least nine dogs in orbit. And at least that many made suborbital rocket flights in "unpressurized" cabins, where they were required to wear space suits and oxygen masks.

The first dog in orbit, and most famous "muttnik," as they were often called, was an eleven-pound (5 kg) white female mixed-breed named Laika. For her flight, launched on November 3, 1957, she was sponged with an alcohol solution and combed with a fine-toothed comb. She was daubed with iodine and sprinkled with an antiseptic powder where electrodes would be attached to her body. Then, dressed in a special harness, she was put into a pressurized cabin of the cone-shaped *Sputnik II*.

The cabin had many instruments to provide life support for Laika and to transmit data back to earth.

Liftoff and ascent caused no ill effects. In-flight cameras showed that Laika moved, barked, and ate food from an automatic dispenser. The electrodes attached to her body recorded her heartbeat and breath rate, which appeared normal. She was the first living creature ever to go into orbit around the earth, and she proved that animals could live safely in a weightless condition. Laika remained in orbit for a week.

The survival of living creatures in weightlessness

Laika in her Sputnik II *capsule*

was now assured. The next question was, would all life-support systems of the spacecraft function safely enough for a human being to be launched into space? Again, animals would be used for test flights.

On August 19, 1960, *Sputnik V* took off with two dogs, named Strelka and Belka, aboard. Both the dogs selected were even-tempered, and both would be checked in flight by the instruments attached to them and by video cameras that recorded how they behaved and felt. The two dogs were not the only passengers. Accompanying them were forty mice, two rats, and some forms of plant life. After eighteen orbits all returned safely.

Although the mission seemed to show that the craft was worthy and safe for a human to try, the craft's

Belka became a celebrity after her return to earth. She is seen here barking into the microphone in the studio of a Moscow radio station.

designer still was not satisfied. Therefore another spacecraft, *Sputnik VI,* was launched on December 1, 1960, to make further tests. The passengers this time were two dogs, Pchelka and Mushka. Mice, insects, and plant life were also aboard. But the craft's trajectory (path) was faulty, and it was destroyed upon reentering the atmosphere.

The condition that caused this setback was corrected and the Soviets pressed on, launching yet another craft, *Sputnik IX,* on March 9, 1961. It carried a dog, Chernushka, along with guinea pigs and mice. They completed one orbit and returned safely.

But the Soviet State Commission still said no to manned flight. It was decided that one more test flight was needed, and *Sputnik X* went up on March 25, 1961, carrying a dog named Zvezdochka. Her flight

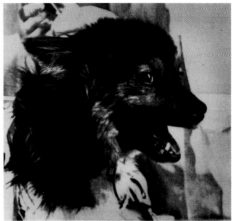

In 1966 Soviet space dogs Veterok (left) and Ugolyok spent three weeks in earth orbit during a flight that took them deeper into space than humans had ever ventured.

finally assured the authorities that all systems of the craft were functioning well. It was now safe enough for a cosmonaut (Soviet astronaut) to be launched into space.

Seventeen days later, the Soviet State Commission gave the go-ahead for "the world's first manned space flight on the spaceship *Vostok* for 12 April, 1961." Major Yuri Gagarin was the cosmonaut chosen for the honor. His flight of one orbit, 108 minutes long, was safe and successful.

After reentry, the Soviet space capsules were par-

21

achuted to solid land, not to the ocean as the American capsules would be.

Five years later the Soviet spaceship *Kosmos 110* set a record. In the craft were two dogs, Ugolyok and Veterok. They spent 22 days in space and completed 330 orbits!

Other countries conducted animal experiments, too. But their space activities were far fewer than those of the Americans and Soviets.

THE AMERICAN MONKEYNAUTS

Instead of using trained dogs for major space experiments, the United States used primates. Monkeys and apes of all kinds are more similar to human beings than other animals. Also, they are good at using their hands. Those taking part in the experiments were often called "monkeynauts."

One of the first American tests of the effects of zero-g, or weightlessness, was made with the Aerobee rocket in the 1940s. A special capsule to hold animals was built. Two young monkeys and two white mice made the flight. The mice were placed in a clear plastic ball, and the monkeys were fastened to foam-rubber couches. The monkeys were sedated so they wouldn't pull free from the instruments fastened to their bodies, which monitored their heartbeat and breathing. Films taken during the flight showed that the mice were a little confused by the weightlessness, but the monkeys seemed unaffected by the experience. All the animals returned safely. As soon as the monkeys were released from the capsule, one of them greedily ate a banana.

Like the Soviet dogs, the monkeys were trained to

A space suit is tried on a test monkey for size.

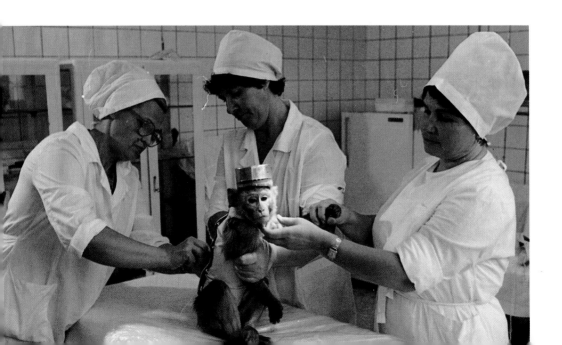

wait patiently for long periods of time. And they had to become accustomed to exposure to great speed, hcat, and vibration.

On June 11, 1948, it is recorded that a rhesus monkey weighing nine pounds (4 kg) was sealed inside a pressurized capsule and sent soaring into space on a V-2 rocket. His name was Albert. Almost a year later, another rhesus monkey, Albert II, was sent up to an altitude of 83 miles (134 km), and lived through an entire flight, also on a V-2 rocket. Both flights ended badly because of parachute trouble.

During the following four years Aerobee and V-2 rockets continued to carry monkeys aloft. The examining doctors reported undisturbed circulation of the blood, normal breathing, and good food digestion. Also, they reported that the monkeys did not seem overly frightened.

On May 22, 1952, the last Aerobee flight was made. Two rhesus monkeys (macaques) and two mice were sent up. It is said that one of the monkeys was called Stratosphere Mike. Their flight ended safely.

After that, live animal rocket research was halted by the United States for five years. Attention was given instead to ballistic missile experiments.

However, in 1953 and 1954, giant balloons carried some monkeys and mice in capsules to great heights to study the effects of radiation. The heavy

An Air Force officer holds a monkey recovered safely from an Aerobee rocket. The vessel was fired during a series of rocket experiments that sent monkeys 80 miles (128.7 km) high into the sky.

cosmic rays affected some of the black mice—in a few weeks they turned gray. But the monkey tests confirmed that their twenty four hour exposure to radiation in space did not create severe health hazards.

A new mission, Project Mercury, was already under way in preparation for manned flight while other animal spacecraft experiments were taking place. An Army Jupiter rocket was launched from Cape Canaveral, Florida, on December 13, 1958. It carried a small squirrel monkey named Old Reliable. Sensors taped to his body recorded his heartbeat, breathing, and blood pressure. Test results showed that he did not suffer in flight. Old Reliable rode in the nose cone and performed well on the flight.

The next notable "monkeynaut" flight took place on May 28, 1959. Two female monkeys were companions on a 10,000 mile (16,000 km)-an-hour ride to an altitude of 300 miles (483 km) in an Army Jupiter missile. One was a seven-pound (3.18 kg) rhesus monkey named Able, born in America and trained by the Army. The other was a tiny two-year-old squirrel monkey, born in Peru and trained at the Naval School of Medicine in Pensacola, Florida. The squirrel monkey was called Miss Baker and weighed only one pound (.45 kg).

According to information recorded through her sensors, Miss Baker was a little startled at the time of

(Above) Miss Baker (top) and Able are shown after both were recovered from the nose cone of the Army Jupiter missile they traveled in during a historic space flight in May 1959. (Facing page) Sea crewmen lift the "biopack" (container) from which Miss Sam (inset) was recovered in good condition. The lower part of the space capsule is shown below the biopack.

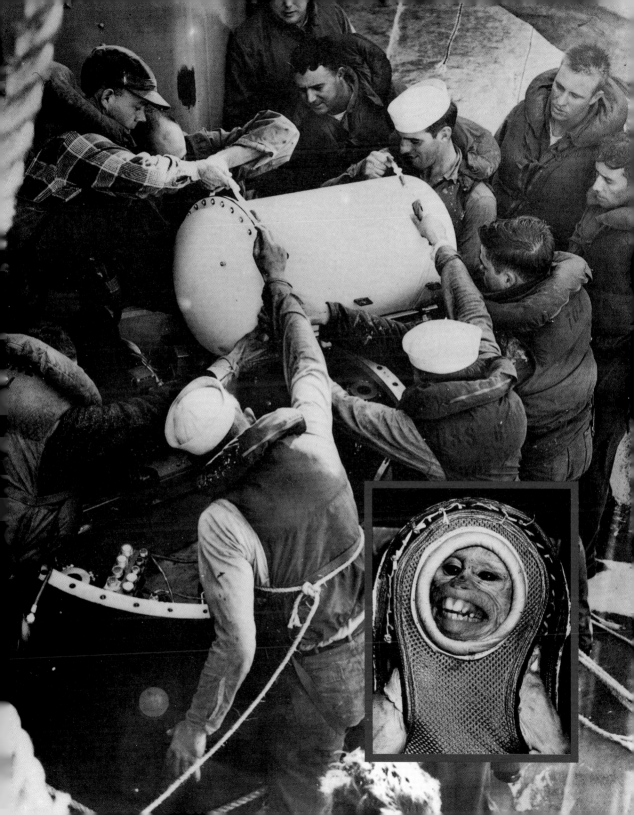

lift-off. Other than that, all went well, and when the capsule was picked up both Able and Miss Baker were alive and hungry. As the feisty little Miss Baker was taken from the capsule, she bit her rescuer and then devoured a cracker and a banana.

This flight confirmed that animals could survive not only weightlessness, but also the stress caused by liftoff and reentry.

On December 4, 1959, a male rhesus monkey named Sam made a suborbital flight in a Mercury capsule launched from Wallops Island, Virginia. Two months later, on January 21, 1960, Miss Sam, a female rhesus, was sent up from the same place in a Mercury capsule that reached an altitude of 48,900 feet (15 km). Her flight tested the Mercury launch escape system.

As Project Mercury came closer to launching a manned satellite into space, the training of the primates became more rugged. Data from previous animal flights gave positive information about blood pressure, heart and breath rate, digestion, and circulation in zero-g surroundings. Still it was also necessary to know if the human *mind* could function well in the weightlessness of space.

The primates would answer this question, too.

THE AMERICAN ASTROCHIMPS

3

The decade of the 1960s had now begun and the space era was off to a roaring start. It would include some of the most spectacular developments in the conquest of space.

At around this time thirty chimpanzees, born in West Africa, were brought to Holloman Air Force Base in New Mexico. They were enrolled in a training class at the Holloman Aeromedical Research Laboratory. The scientists there had trained the monkeys that had flown in the V-2 and Aerobee rockets.

Often called "astrochimps," the chimpanzees all had numbers instead of names. During training they were caged. Over and over again they tried to escape, but the veterinarians were patient and kind. Like all the animals who trained before them, the chimps had to become accustomed to things that were strange to them, like flying at great speed. And they had to learn how it felt to be weightless and how to function in that state. They had to learn to tolerate heat and loud noises.

As part of their training they were placed in a centrifuge, where everything is forced away from the middle while turning rapidly. The centrifuge experience gives the same effect the animal would feel at liftoff, when it is pushed hard against the back of the couch seat. At launching the subject is forced back because of the "escape velocity," the great speed

This chimpanzee, trained at the Holloman Air Force Base, participated in a sixteen-minute flight test in preparation for NASA's manned orbital flight program, Project Mercury.

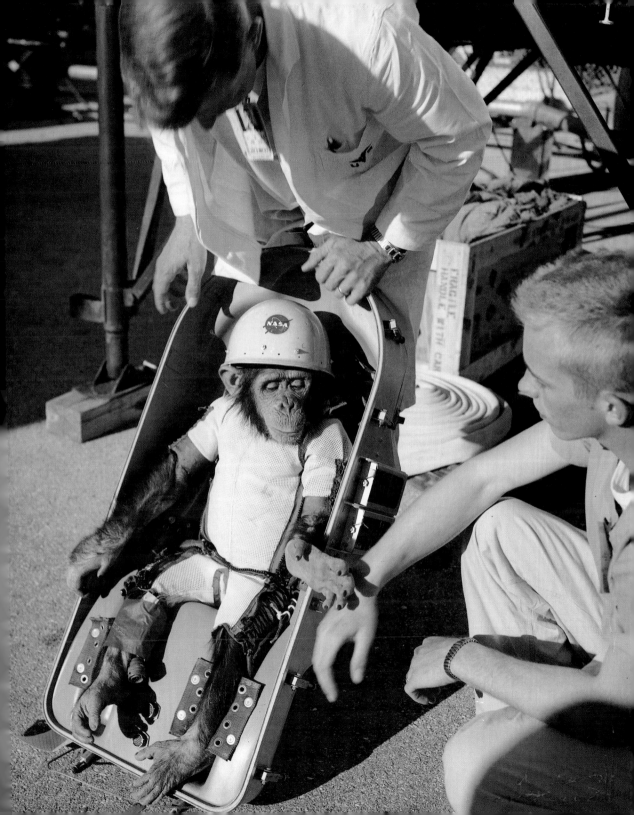

needed to break free of gravity and pierce the atmosphere.

The chimpanzees learned quickly and well, but they weren't only going to take a ride through space as did their predecessors. They were also going to perform tasks in flight.

The chimps were trained to pull a right-hand lever when a white light showed and a left-hand lever when a blue light appeared. They learned to wait for twenty seconds after a green light came on before pressing a lever for a sip of water. To get a banana-flavored tablet they had to pull a lever fifty times.

Small electric pads were wired to the soles of the chimpanzees' feet. If they did not answer the signals correctly, a tiny tingling in their feet told them to try again.

For nine months the chimpanzees practiced.

(Top) Chimpanzees Duane, Jim, and Chu pose in their space capsules as they undergo training for future flights in space. (Bottom) Chatter, another chimpanzee, beams proudly as he holds a photograph of his cousin Ham.

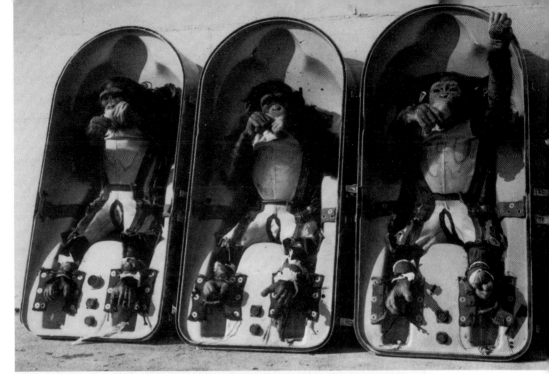

Finally, in November 1960, the six best-trained animals, with twenty veterinarians in attendance, were taken to Cape Canaveral, Florida.

One of the six chimpanzees would be chosen for a most important flight—to precede a person going into space. Number 65 was selected. He was four years old, weighed 37 pounds (16.8 kg), and was bright and alert but quiet-tempered. He had to practice up until the night before the flight. Then he was given the name Ham—taken from the initials of the first three words of the Holloman Aerospace Medical Center.

Ham wore a nylon mesh harness and was placed on a couch in the capsule of *Mercury 2* on January 31, 1961. He waited patiently for lift-off. Then swoosh, he was up and away, pressed hard against the couch. He watched the panel and pulled the right-hand lever when the white lights came on. Then he pulled a left-hand lever when he saw the blue lights. His flight

(Top) A close-up view of the Mercury *space capsule that rocketed Ham into space. (Bottom) Upon touchdown, the astrochimp was awarded a big red apple for a job well done.*

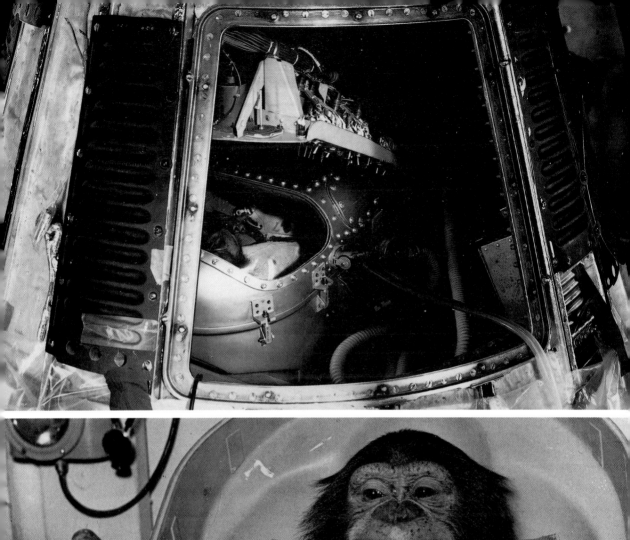

lasted only sixteen and one-half minutes, but it was considered very successful. Ham performed well.

Shortly afterward, on May 5, 1961, an American astronaut, Navy Commander Alan Shepard, manned a suborbital flight. It was the *Mercury 3* mission and the capsule was named *Freedom 7,* in honor of the original seven astronauts.

Shepard's flight was much the same as Ham's, a quick ride into space and back to earth. He splashed down in the ocean just as Ham did.

Now it was time to go into full orbit around the earth. Again a chimpanzee was chosen to precede a manned flight. This time Number 81 was picked. He was the brightest, but also the most unmanageable of the lot. He had bitten, clawed, and spit at his trainers, but he had learned the fastest and the most thoroughly. His ape fingers flew over the levers. Unlike the friendly Ham, Number 81 was nasty and feisty. At one time during his training, he became so incorrigible he had to be isolated in a box. After a week all by himself, he behaved better.

Right before his flight, Number 81 was named Enos, which means "man" in Hebrew. Enos was prepared and dressed the same way Ham had been. But their flights were very different. Ham only had to pull the levers when the white and blue lights showed. Enos had to use all the lessons he learned. He pulled

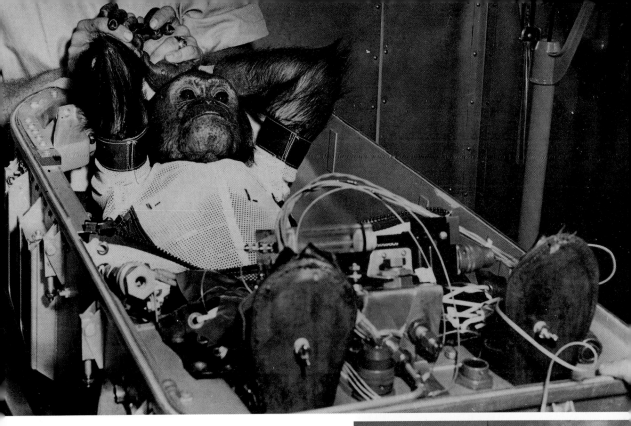

(Right) The Mercury Atlas-5 craft carrying the five-and-a-half-year-old chimp Enos (above) rises from the launchpad at Cape Canaveral in 1961.

levers for sips of water and banana-flavored tablets, which came to him through tubes positioned near his mouth. He also pulled levers under different symbols—circles, squares, and triangles—to test his intelligence.

Enos went through it all with flying colors. However, because of mechanical trouble some of his tasks, though he did them correctly, did not bring the right results. Instead of sips of water or banana-flavored tablets, Enos received the tinglings in his feet. The capsule had to be returned to earth after only two orbits instead of the three that were planned. Nevertheless, the flight was considered successful. The mechanism that malfunctioned could be corrected. Most important, Enos returned safely.

Three months later a historic moment occurred. On February 20, 1962, an American astronaut, Marine Lieutenant John Glenn, manned the first American

After a valiant performance in space, where he pressed the right buttons but got the wrong responses, an angry Enos is escorted off a plane upon his return.

flight in orbit around the earth. He completed three orbits. The mission was *Mercury 6* and the capsule was called *Friendship 7*.

At this point, both the United States and the Soviet Union stopped using animals to test manned spacecraft. However, both nations continued to conduct animal-in-space tests on the effects of weightlessness. If humans were to stay in space for an extended length of time, would they be as unaffected by weightlessness as those who had survived the shorter trips? And if space stations would ever be built, could human beings live in them safely?

LOWER LIFE-FORMS AND EXPERIMENT RESULTS

4

In 1966 NASA (National Aeronautics and Space Administration) started a program called Biosatellite. It was conducted to learn what effects weightlessness and radioactivity would have on living organisms after long periods of time.

The program was divided into three parts, namely *Biosatellite 1, 2, 3*. *Biosatellite 1* did not succeed because of trouble at recovery time. However, *Biosatellite 2* did succeed. It was launched on September 7, 1967, carrying a number of lower life-forms—bacteria, molds, plants, fruit flies, wasps, and beetles. The mission lasted forty-five hours and excellent information was gained. On recovery, the condition of the specimens was good.

Biosatellite 3 orbited on June 28, 1969. This time the capsule carried a fifteen-pound (6.8 kg) male primate named Bonny, equipped with sensors. Bonny became ill, so the thirty-day mission was ended after nine days. Some satisfactory data was obtained, but not as much as was hoped for because of the shortened flight.

Another experiment was begun on November 9, 1970, when two bullfrogs were sent into orbit. They went up in a Scout launch vehicle from NASA's Wallops Station, Virginia. The project was to gain information on the otolith, a part of the inner ear that de-

A Biosatellite vessel (inset) carried Bonny for his month-long voyage. Sensors implanted in the primate's body told scientists how prolonged weightlessness in space affected the animal's mental and emotional state.

termines a person's equilibrium, or balance. Why did it help people keep their balance? In frogs the otolith is much like that in the inner ear of a human being. At first the frogs were a little disoriented, but they regained their balance within seventy-two hours. The launch vessel re-entered the earth's atmosphere three months later, but was never recovered.

On through the 1980s scientists continued to study the weightlessness problem. Could all body processes adjust easily to the weightless condition of space? For instance, space authorities wanted to be sure that bone or muscle weakening, if it occurred, could be overcome.

So animal experimentation continued for the safety of all human beings launched into space. There had to be ways to do in-flight surgery and to improve the treatment of medical problems in space. Great progress had been made, but life in space is so different from life on earth that it is very important to understand how organisms withstand those differences.

In space stations of the future it will be necessary to provide food for persons on long-term missions. It will also be necessary to know how sickness and accidents in space can be treated.

One experiment was conducted to learn how plant roots would develop in a place without gravity. No differences in development occurred.

Then on March 13, 1989, several chicken em-

46

bryos (fertilized eggs) were sent up on the space shuttle *Discovery* to find out if they would hatch after a spell of weightlessness. When returned to earth, some of the eggs hatched normally; others did not but for reasons not caused by the flight. One of those that hatched was a hen, which was named Discovery after the shuttle.

An experiment dealing with bone healing was conducted at the same time. For this a rat was chosen. A sliver was taken from a non-weight-bearing bone. The rat returned to earth safely. No troublesome effects were reported; the bone healed normally.

The animals and other biological forms not only helped to assure the safety of the astronauts, animal research gave us many other benefits as well.

NASA states its "biomedical program has generated valuable 'spin-offs' with medical applications for humans." Among these devices are:

• A Programmable Implantable Medication System (PIMS) used for the computer-directed delivery of medication such as insulin for people with diabetes.

• A portable medical status and treatment system for treating heart-attack victims who are out of reach of a hospital.

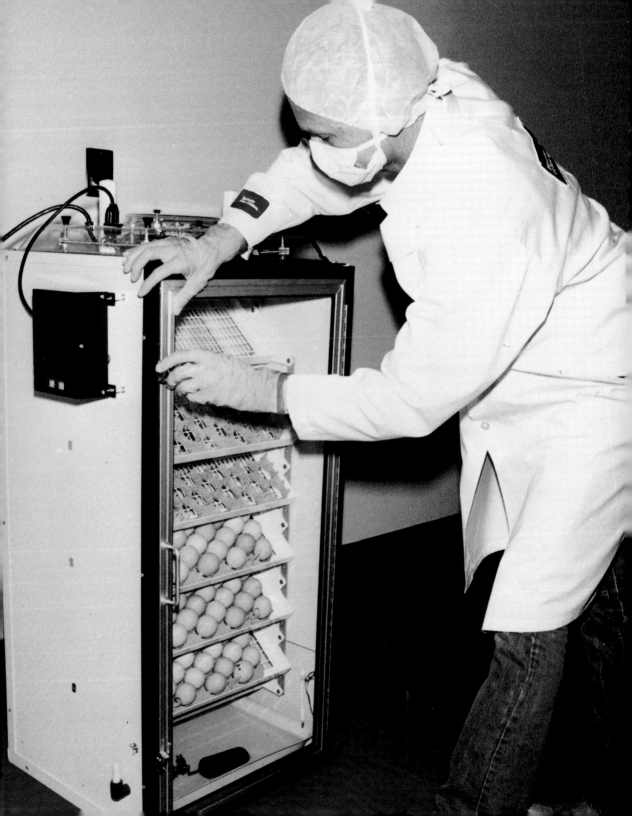

(Facing page) The "Chicken Embryo Development in Space" experiment's aim was to study whether or not spaceflight affected the growth of fertilized chicken embryos. (Above) One of the Biosatellite experiments examined the environmental effects of spaceflight on a healing rat bone.

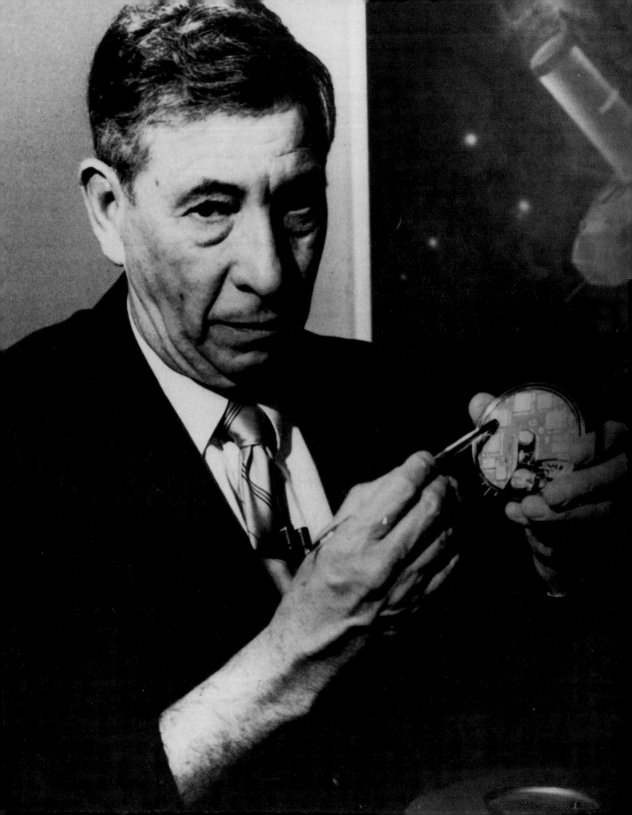

- A human tissue stimulator, an implantable device to help people suffering from chronic pain.

- An automatic implantable defibrillator, which helps to prevent cardiac arrest.

- A programmable cardiac pacemaker.

- An intercranial transducer which can be put into the head of an injured person to measure pressure on the brain.

All these and more came from the knowledge that animals in space helped us to obtain.

Another development, one which helps our knowledge *about* animals, is the "Space-age Collar." It is an electronic package that is placed around the neck of a migratory animal such as the elk. The animal's migration patterns are traced as its electronic signals are picked up by a satellite.

Robert E. Fischell holds up the PIMS unit he invented. When implanted in a diabetic patient, the instrument can deliver precise amounts of insulin over long periods of time.

Of course, many space studies did not involve animals. But animals led the way. They helped us learn what was safe and unsafe in space.

However, there has been controversy. Many people are against using animals for experiments of any kind. They love animals and do not want to see them suffer, and rightly so. But according to NASA's policy in the care of its animals, extreme or unneeded suffering was never inflicted on any of them.

NASA's long list of provisions and rules assures us that the animals used for experiments were always kept in very sanitary housing, were well fed and cared for. If anything was done that might cause an animal to endure discomfort or pain, anesthetics were used. Afterwards the greatest attention was paid to ensure a complete healing.

It has been said that when Charles Lindbergh flew the Atlantic in 1927, there was a common fly in the little cockpit of his plane. It kept him company, inasmuch as it was something else alive. And that counted during those long, lonely hours above the deep, dark ocean.

No one could dispute the wealth of benefits animals have given to humanity—company, comfort, affection, and the great fund of biological knowledge obtained through their experiments.

This man gently handles a common pocket mouse ideal for space research. The mouse is capable of hibernating on command when its body temperature is lowered.

From the animals that rode the first hot-air balloon, to the fly in Lindbergh's plane, and on to the many animals that blazed the trail into space—we owe them all a great big thank-you.

Able, a rhesus monkeynaut

AFTERWORD

What has happened to the animals used in experiments for the space programs?

We certainly cannot account for all of them. But those who were named in this book, whose fates we could uncover, are told about below.

Albert I and **Albert II** (rhesus monkeys) were lost when their parachutes failed to open on their return to earth.

Stratosphere Mike and companion (rhesus monkeys) survived safe and sound and were sent to

Washington, D.C., to live in the Smithsonian Institution Zoological Park.

Old Reliable (squirrel monkey) survived the flight, but the nose cone of the capsule sank at splashdown and he was never found.

Able (rhesus monkey) survived the flight but died shortly afterwards. She was stuffed and mounted for the National Air and Space museum in Washington, D.C.

Miss Baker (squirrel monkey) survived and lived until 1984 in the Alabama Space Rocket Center in Huntsville, Alabama. She became quite a celebrity to the tourists visiting the Center and was called "The First Lady of Space." She is buried in Huntsville.

Ham (chimpanzee) lived to be twenty-six years old. He was first put into retirement at the Smithsonian Institution Zoological Park in Washington, D.C., where he was a big attraction until 1981. Then he was sent to the North Carolina Zoological Park in Asheboro, North Carolina, where he stayed until his death in January 1983. He was buried at the International Space Hall of Fame in New Mexico.

Enos (chimpanzee) was returned to Holloman Air Force Base after his flight. Unlike Ham, Enos lived only one year after his famous ride. His death in November 1962 was from natural causes.

Bonny (primate) came through the flight, but died shortly afterwards of a heart attack.

Discovery (white hen) was sent to the Lincoln Park Zoo in Chicago, Illinois.

And what became of the "muttniks" that the Soviet Union launched into orbit?

Laika (mixed breed) never came back to earth. She died out there among the stars when the oxygen in her capsule ran out after a week in orbit. The capsule went on orbiting for several months.

Belka and **Strelka** (mixed breeds) survived. Later Strelka delivered a litter of healthy puppies.

Chernuska (mixed breed) returned safely from her trip.

Zvedashka (mixed breed) survived the flight and was recovered.

Ugolyok and **Veterok** (mixed breeds) set a record of 23 days in space, completing 330 orbits. It is not clear what became of them afterward.

SUGGESTED READING

Berger, Melvin. *Space Shuttles and Satellites*. New York: G. P. Putnam's Sons, 1983.

Cottrell, Leonard. *Up in a Balloon*. New York: S. G. Phillips, 1970.

Smith, Howard E. *Daring the Unknown: A History of NASA*. Orlando, Florida: Harcourt Brace Jovanovich, 1987.

Trefil, James S. *Living in Space*. New York: Charles Scribner's Sons, 1981.

INDEX

ABOUT THE AUTHOR

Katherine McGlade Marko is the author of several novels and picture books for young people. Among her books are *Away to Fundy Bay,* a historical novel, and *Whales: Giants of the Sea,* a picture book. In addition, Ms. Marko's articles have appeared in *Jack and Jill, Highlights for Children, Children's Playmate,* and other children's publications. Her work has also been featured in the children's set of *Encyclopaedia Britannica.*

Ms. Marko lives in Elgin, Illinois.